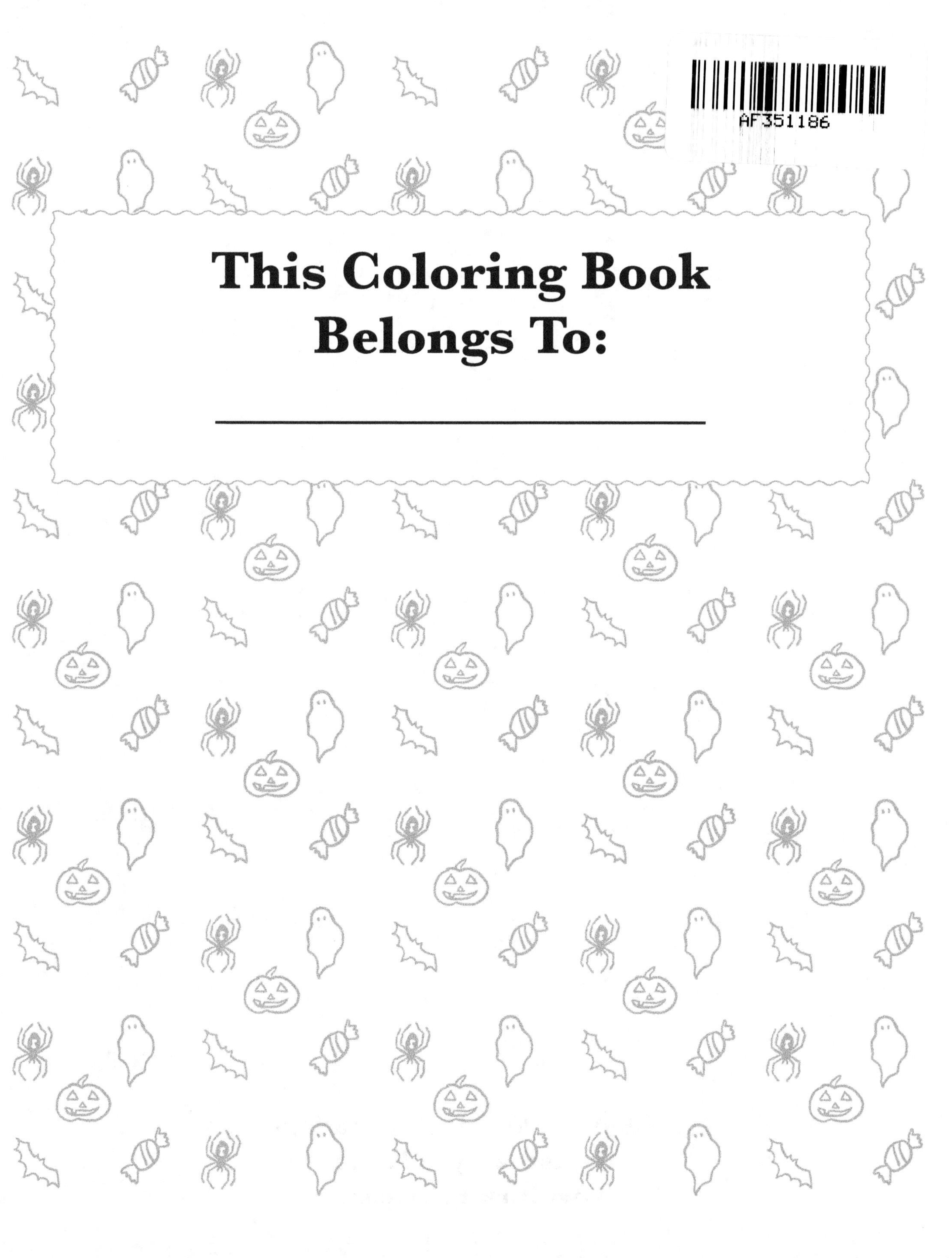

This Coloring Book
Belongs To:

____

Copyright © 2020 DaRK Made, LLC
Denise & Ryan Kester
www.drkmade.com

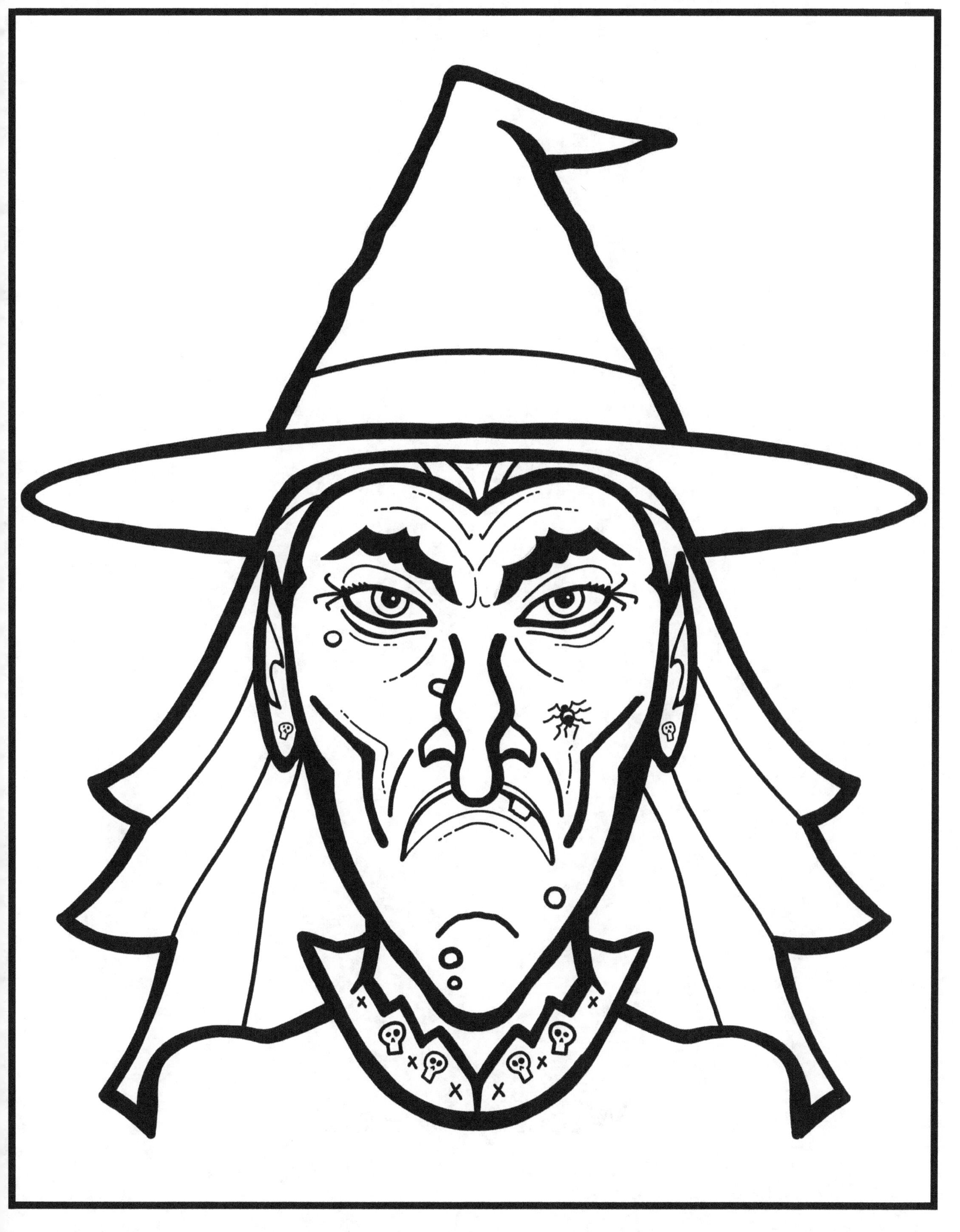

Witchy Witch

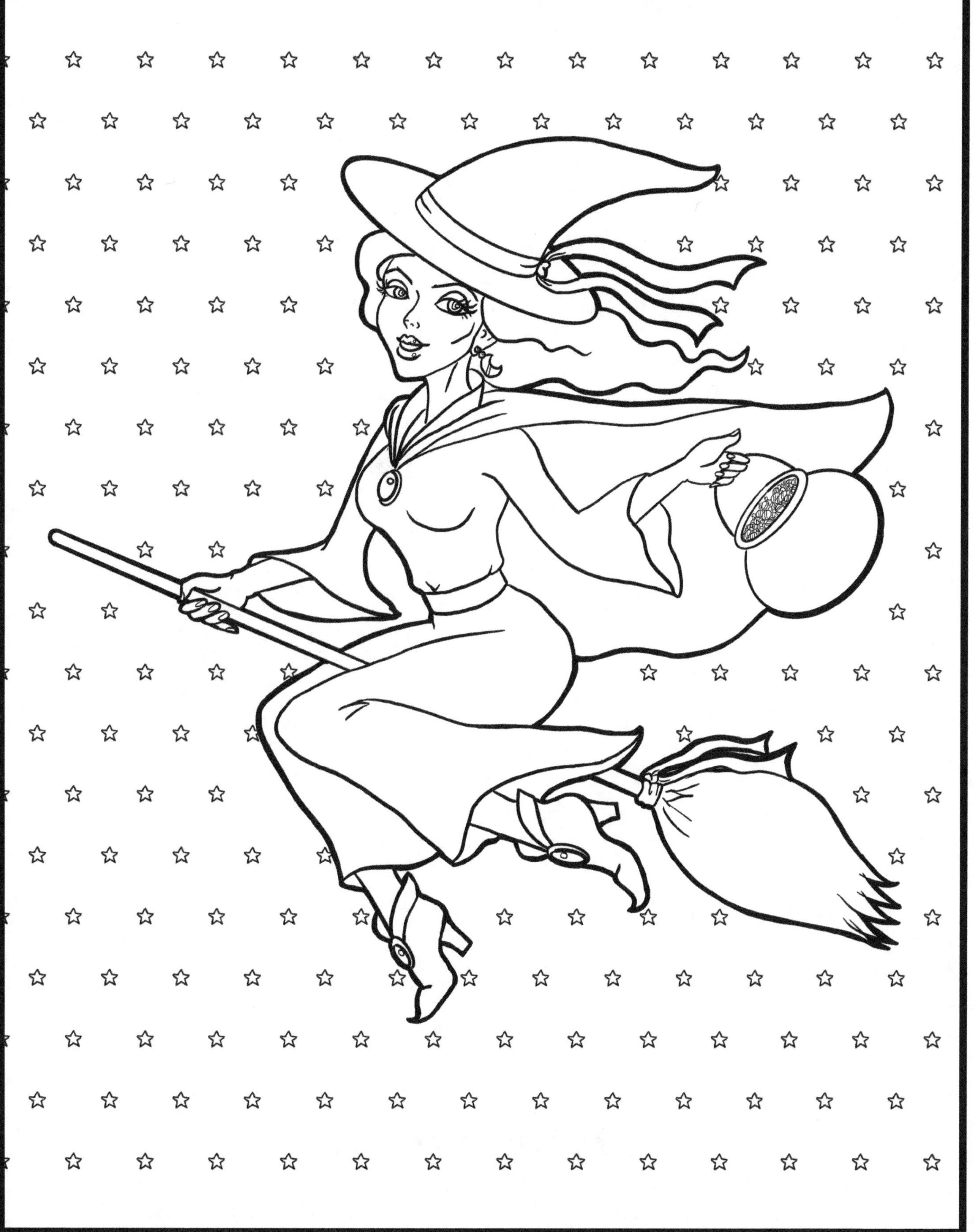

Flying Witch

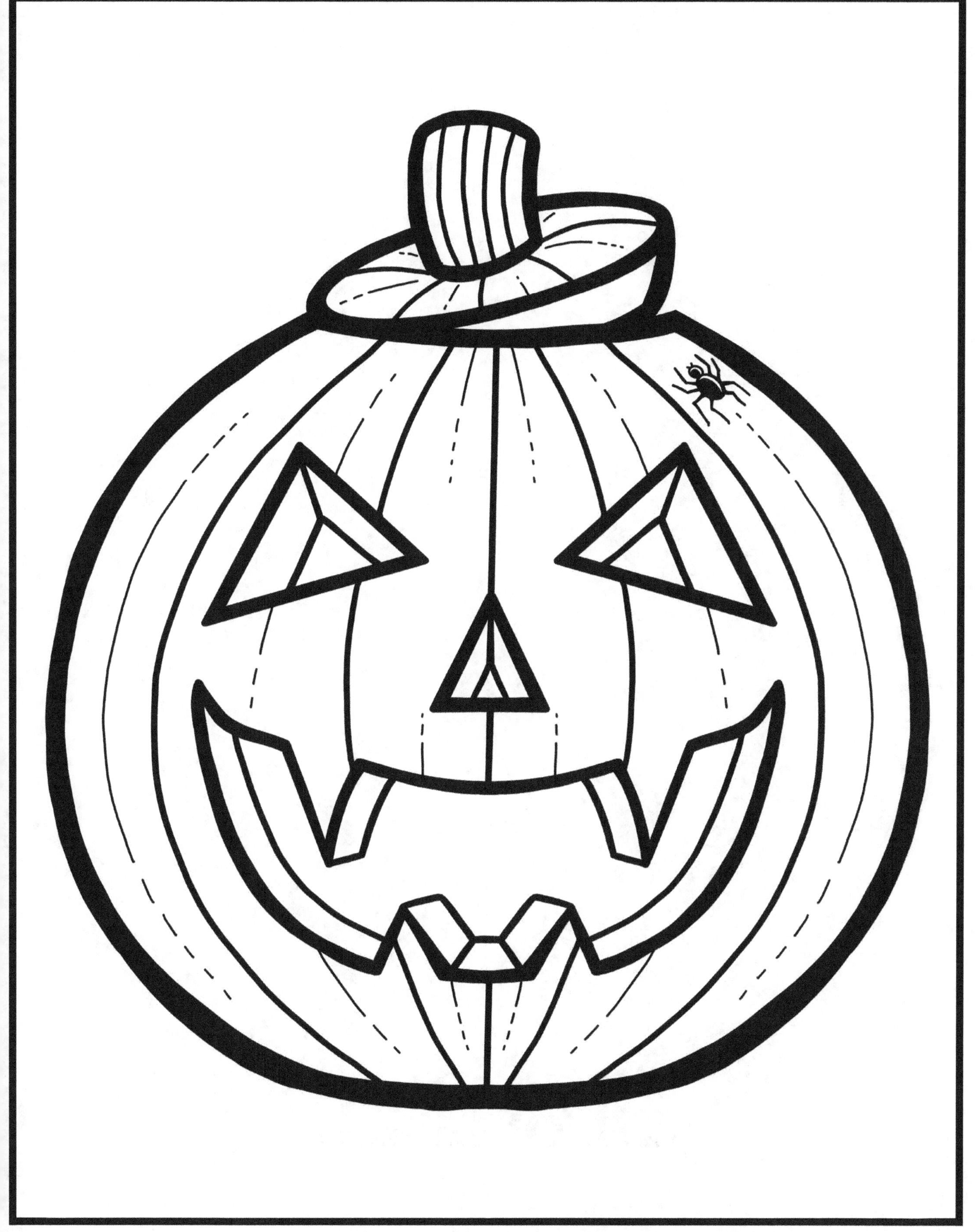

Jack O' Lantern

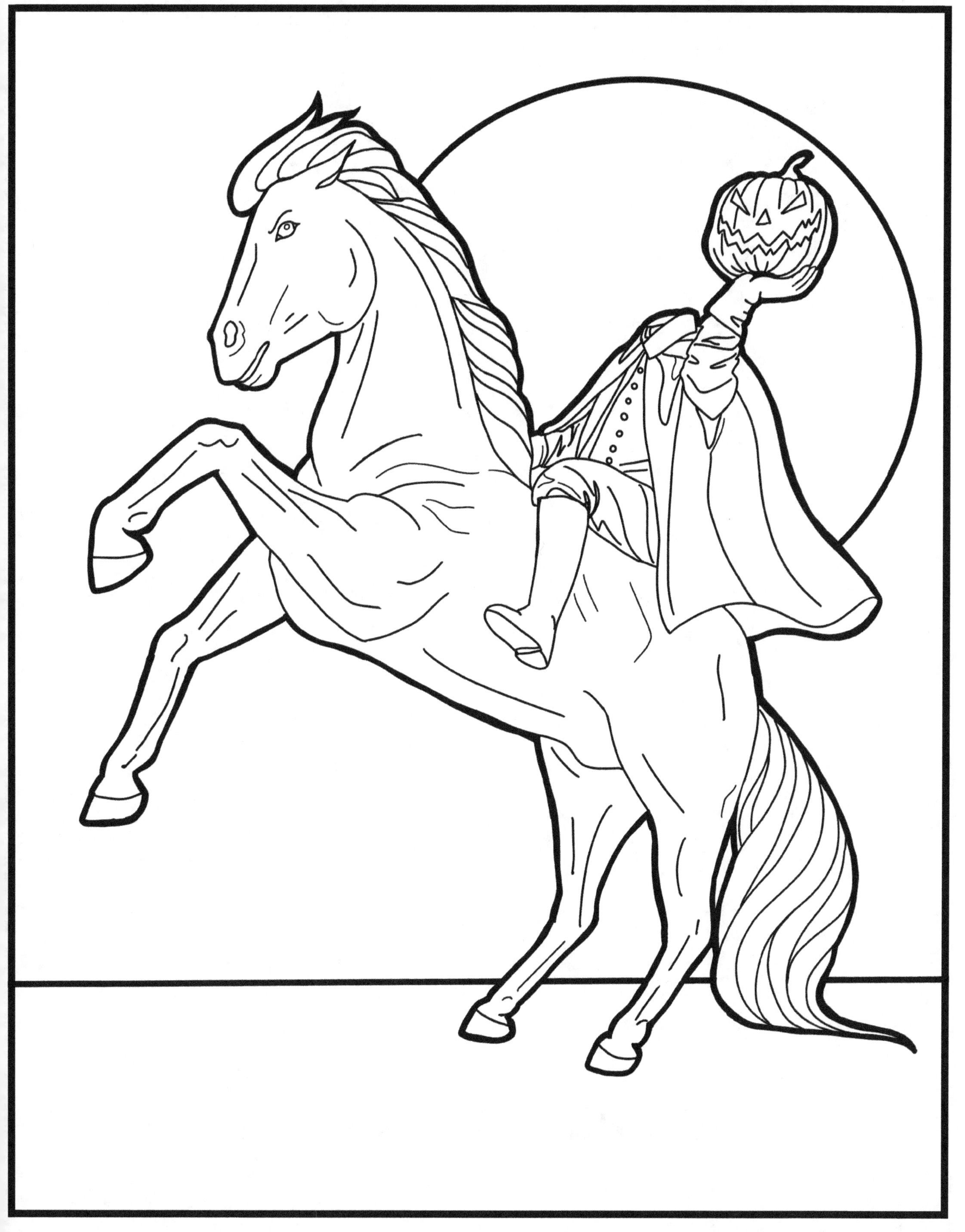

Headless Horseman

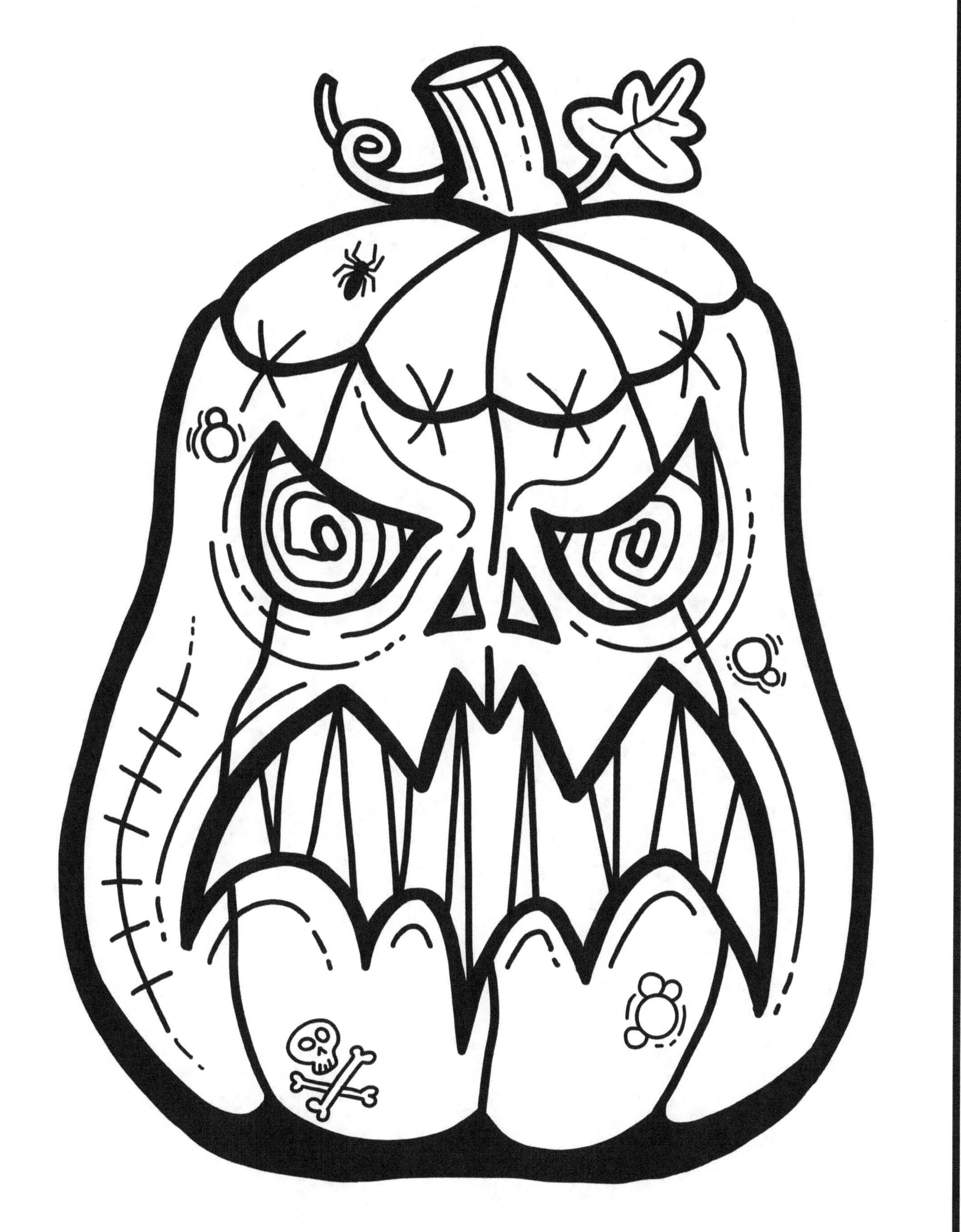

Monster Scarkin

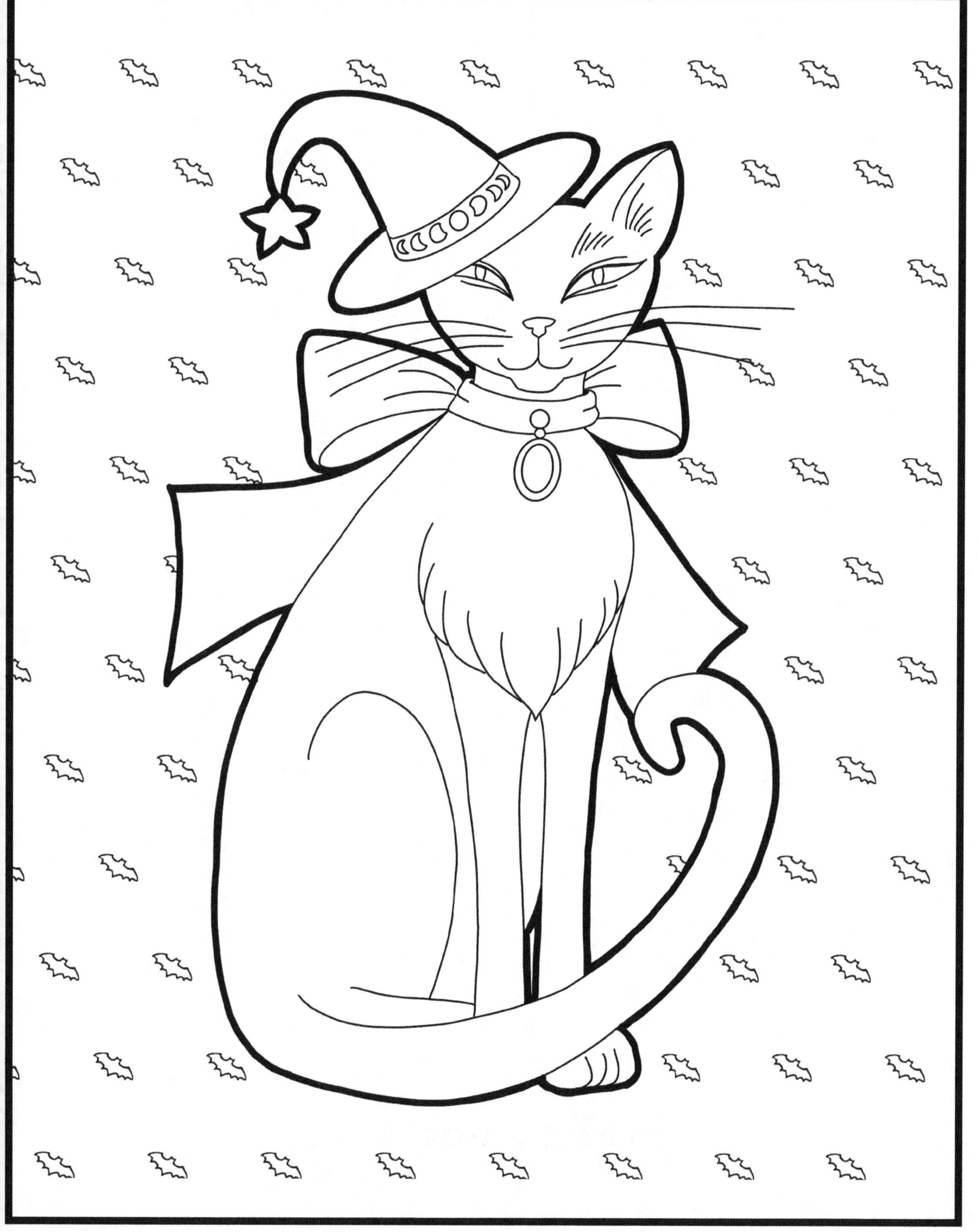

Halloween Cat

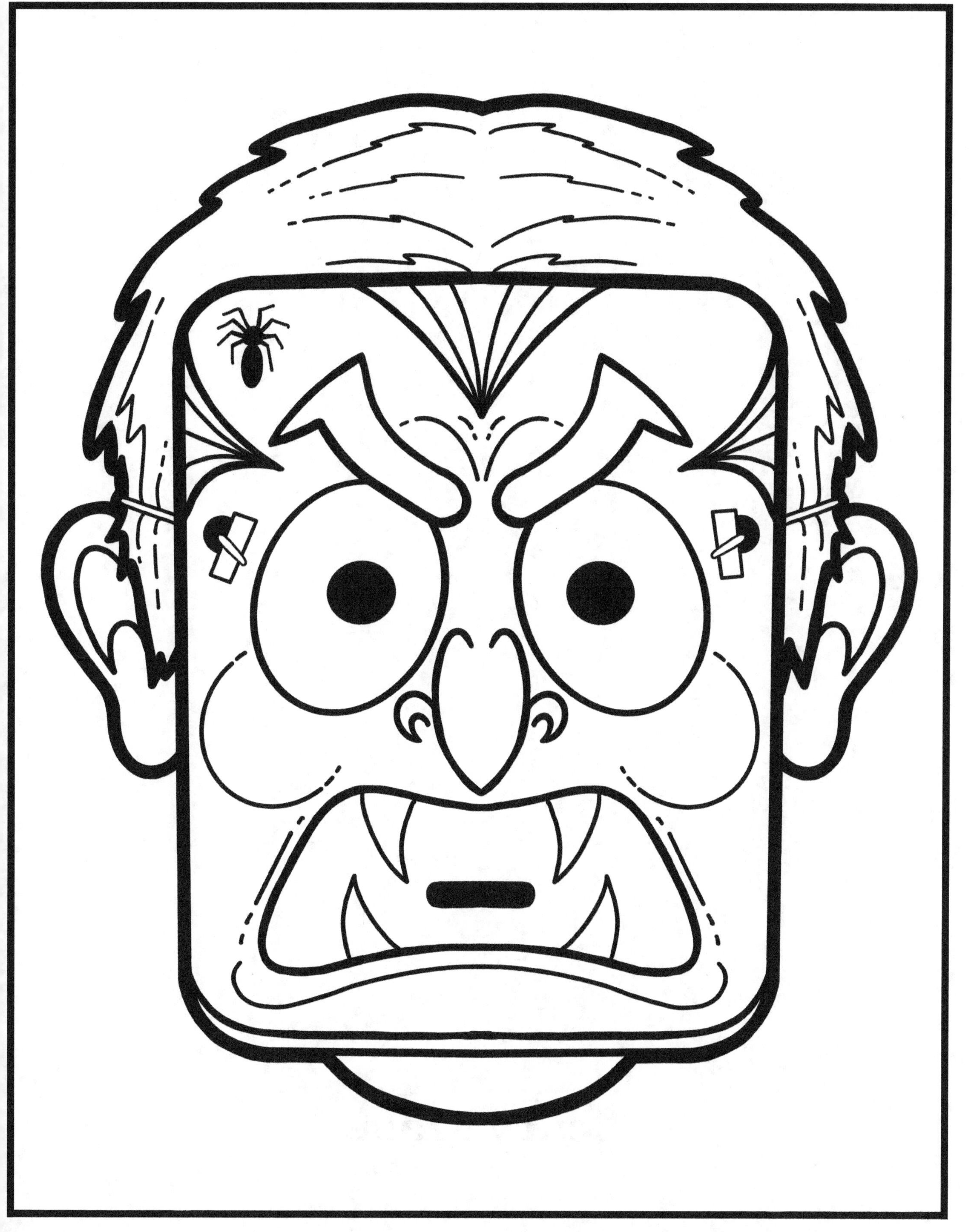

Scary Mask

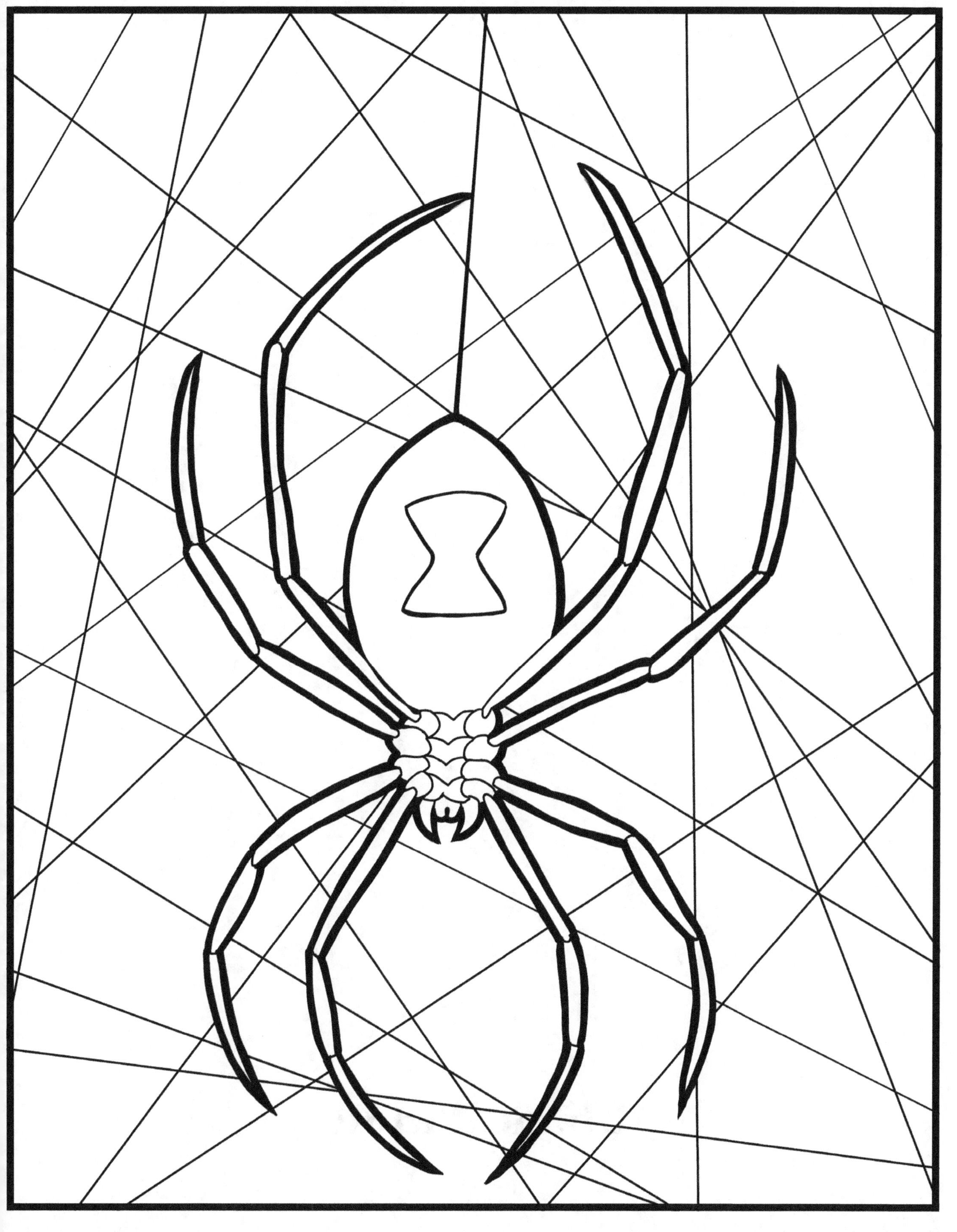

Black Widow

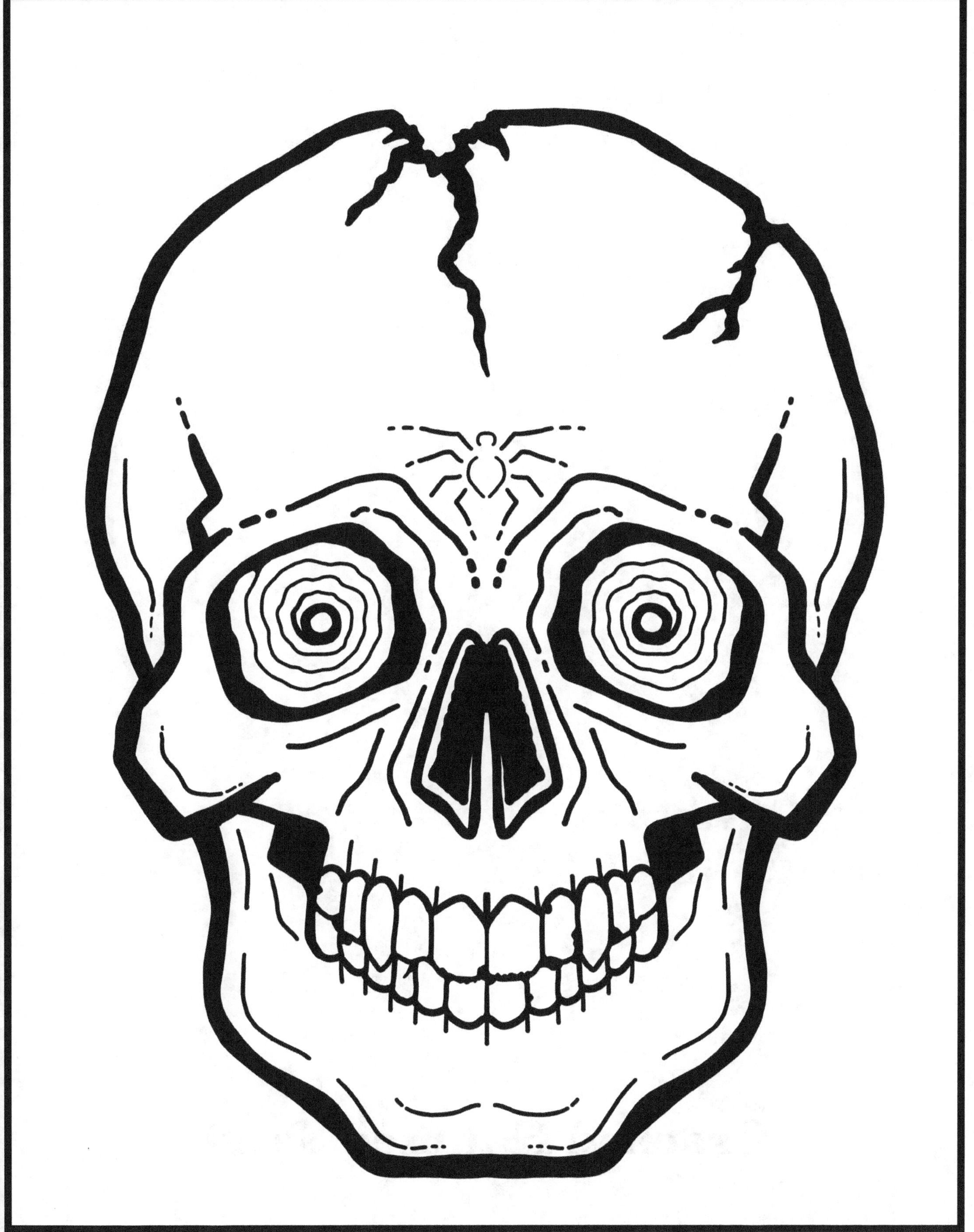

Cracked Haunted Skull

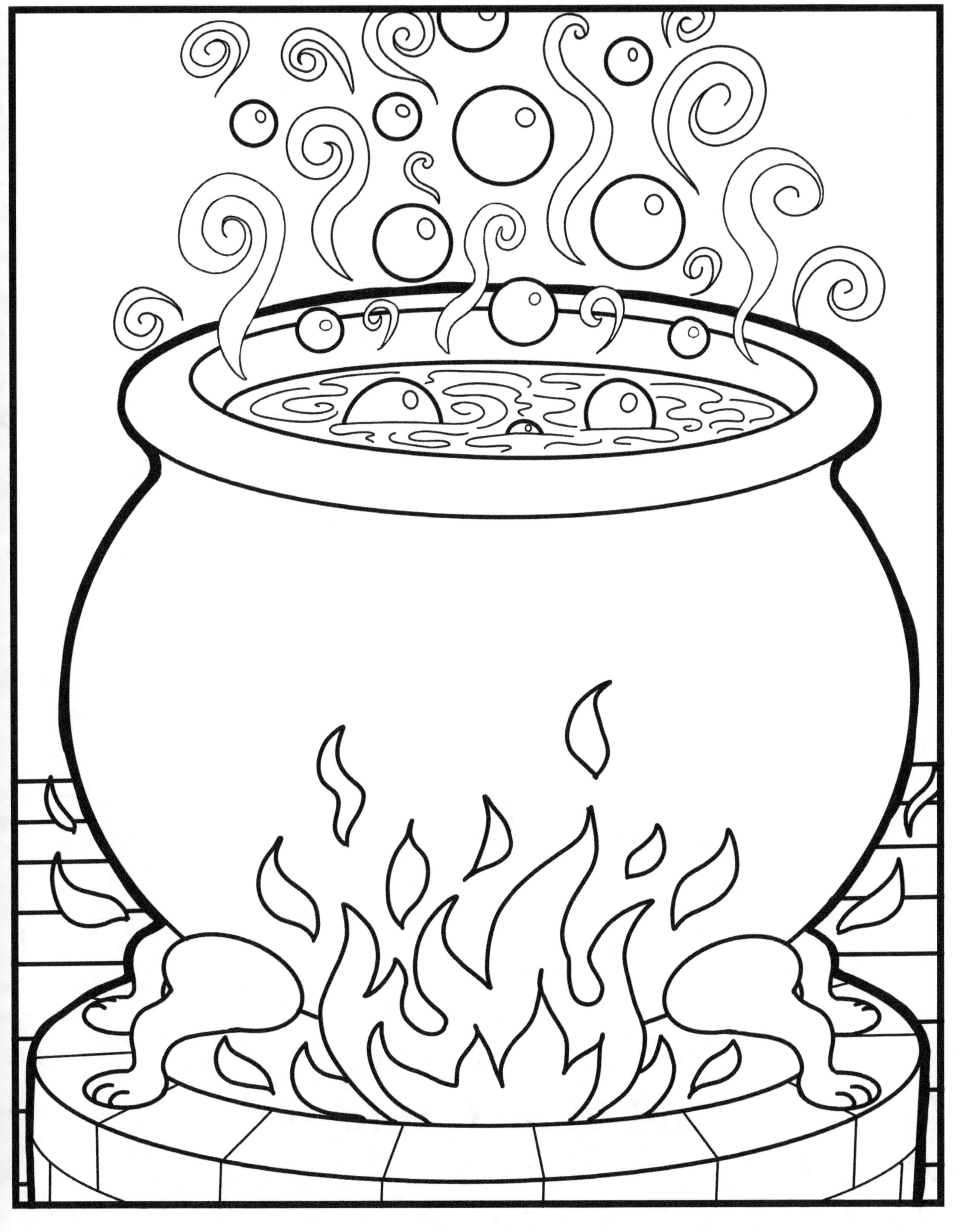

Bubbling Cauldron

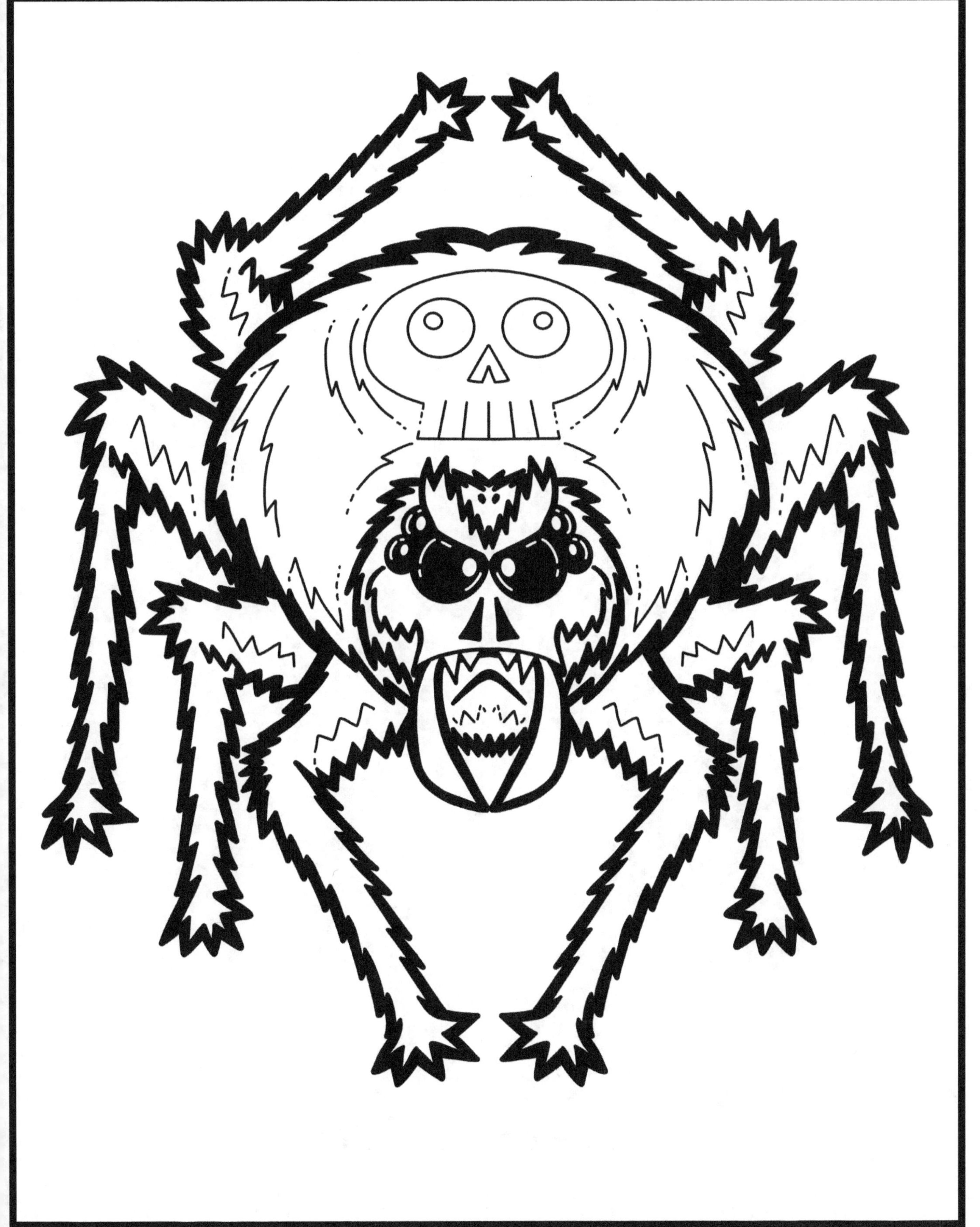

Monster Spider

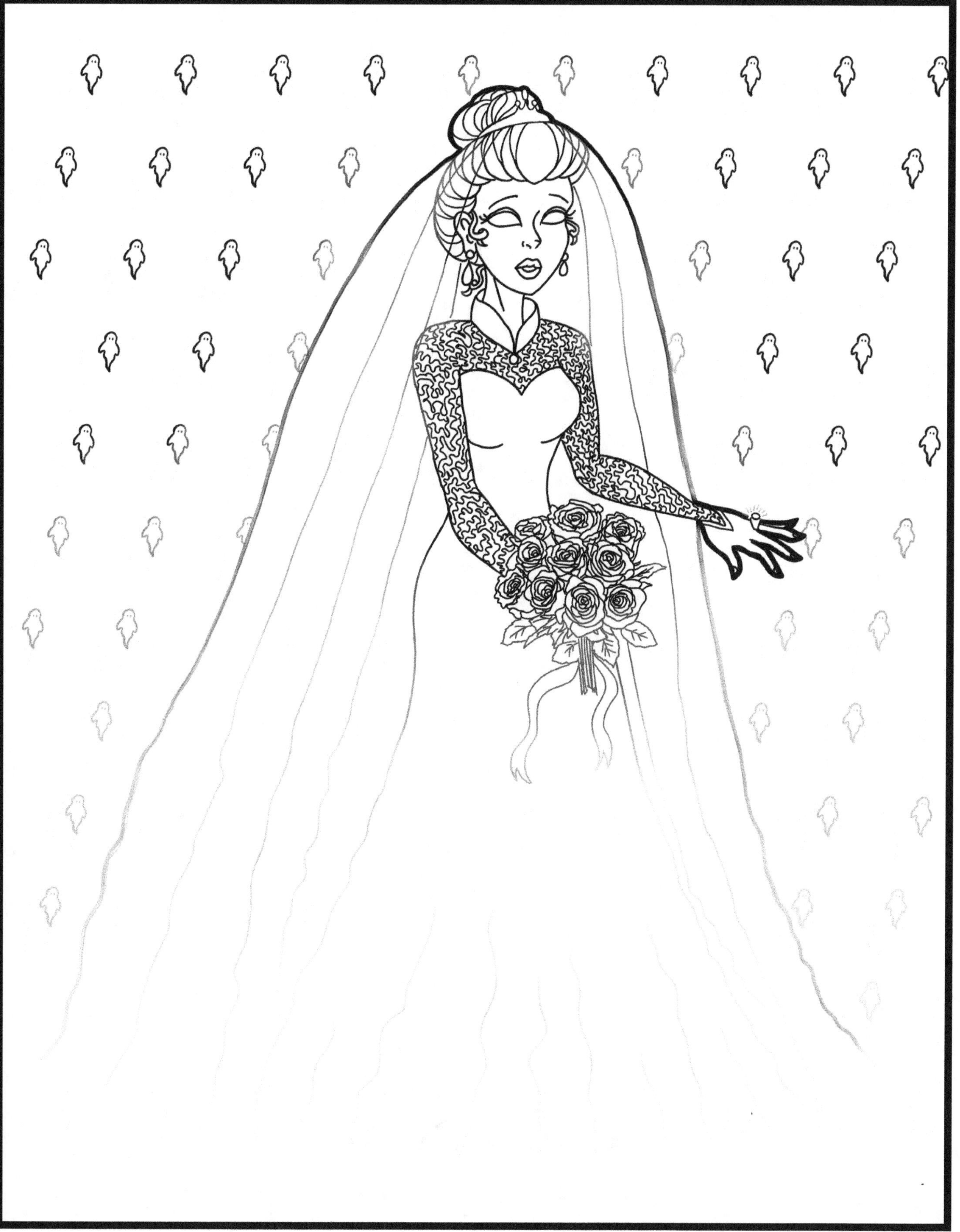

Ghost Bride

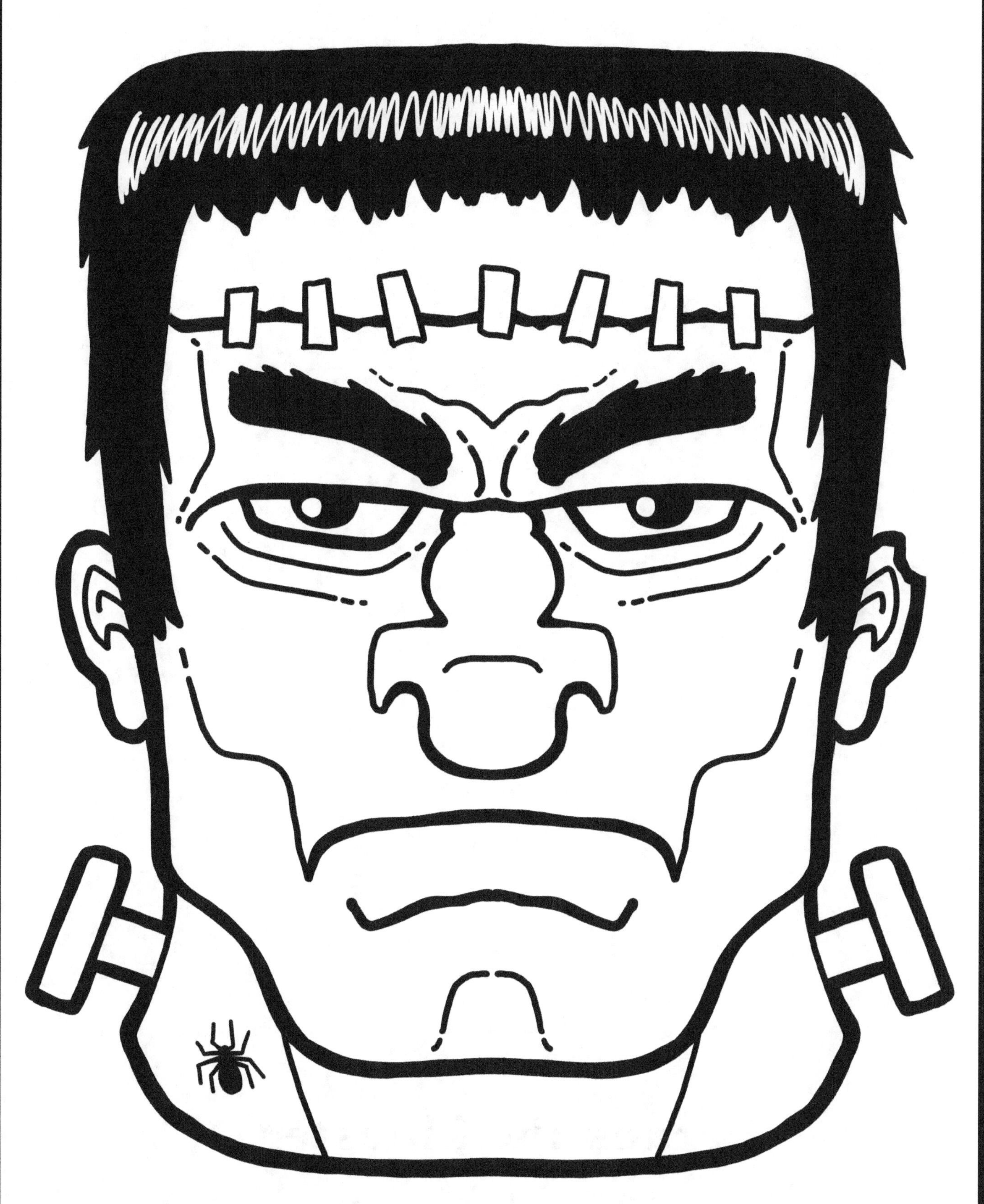

Frank the Monster

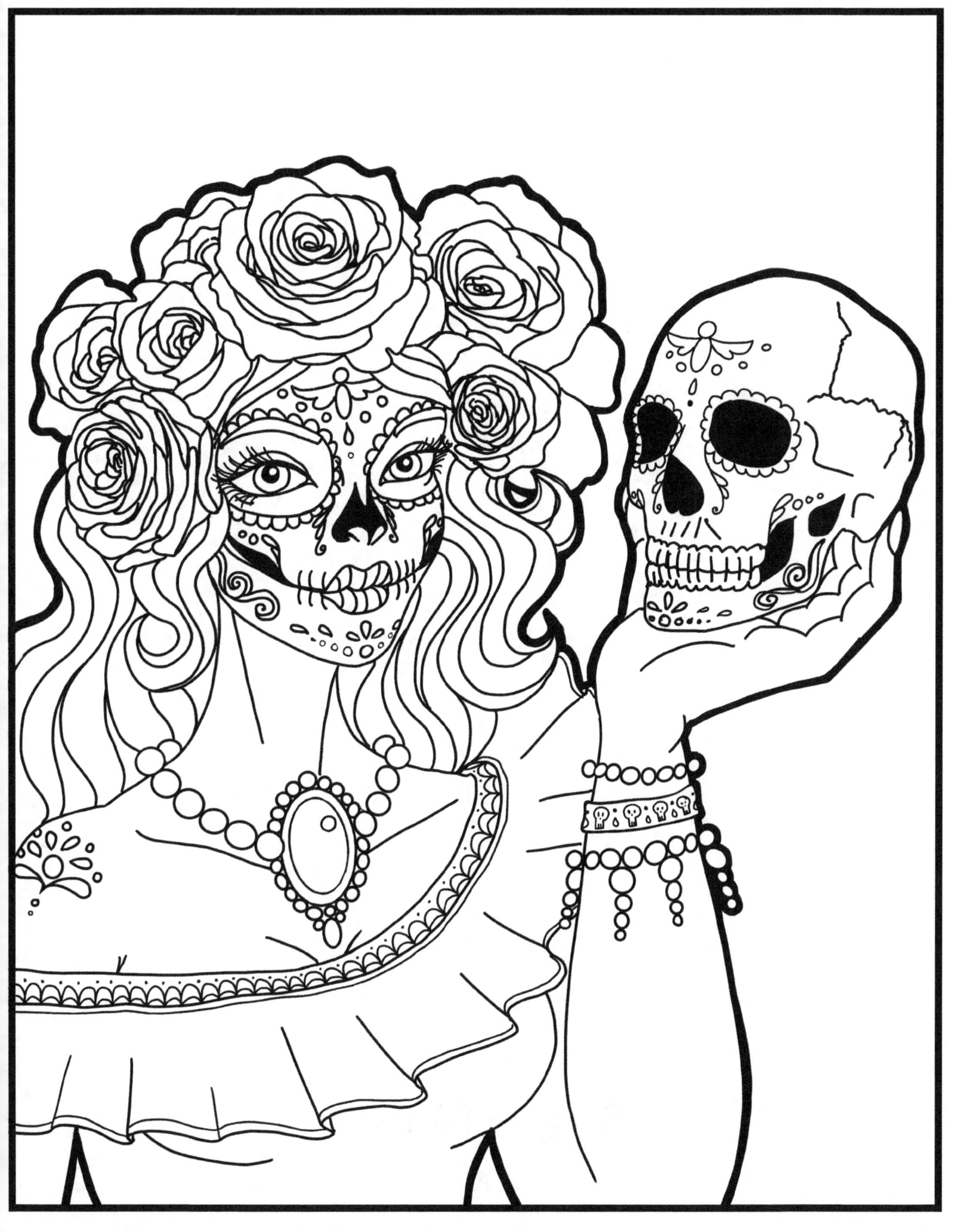

Sugar Skulls

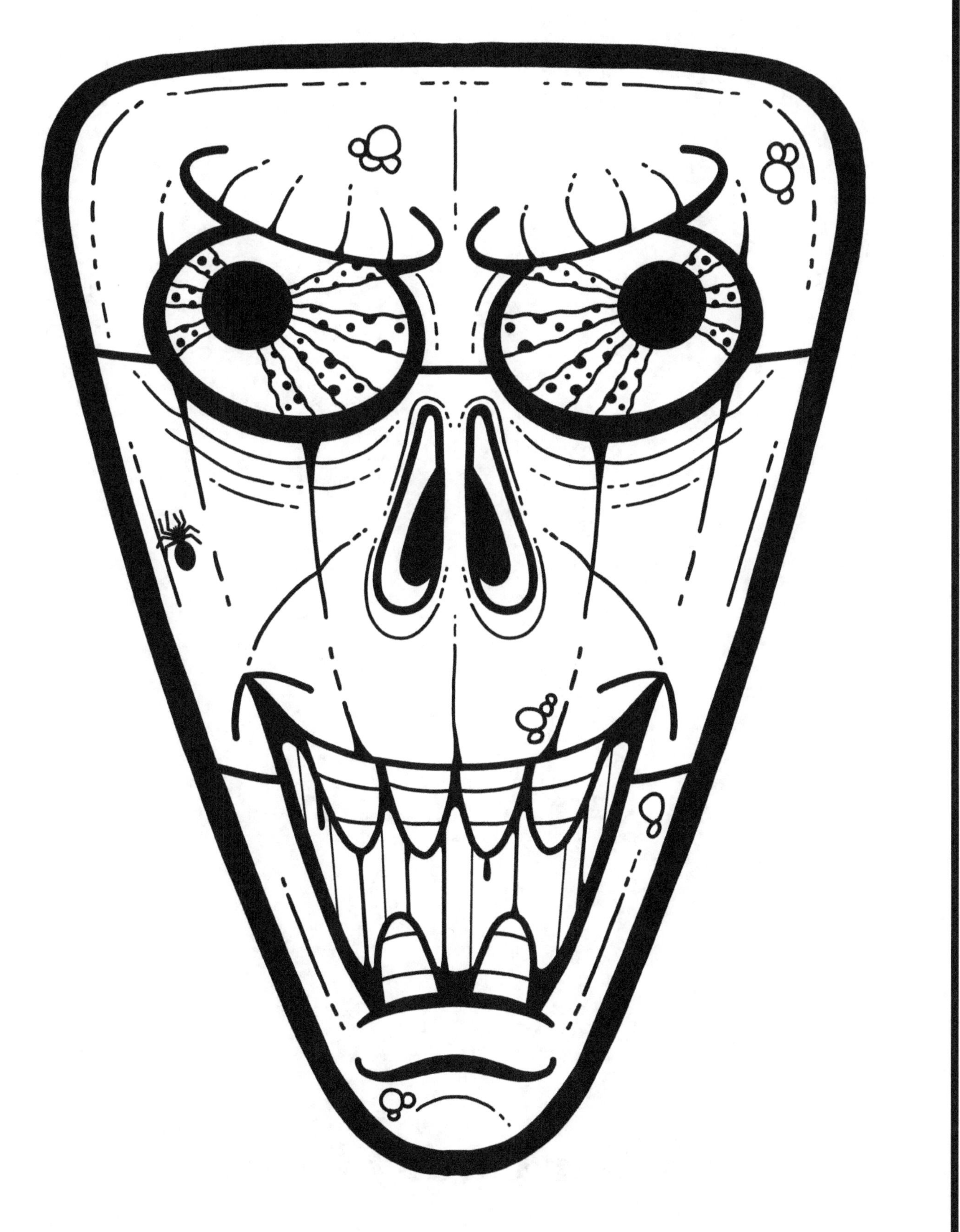

Killer Candy Corn

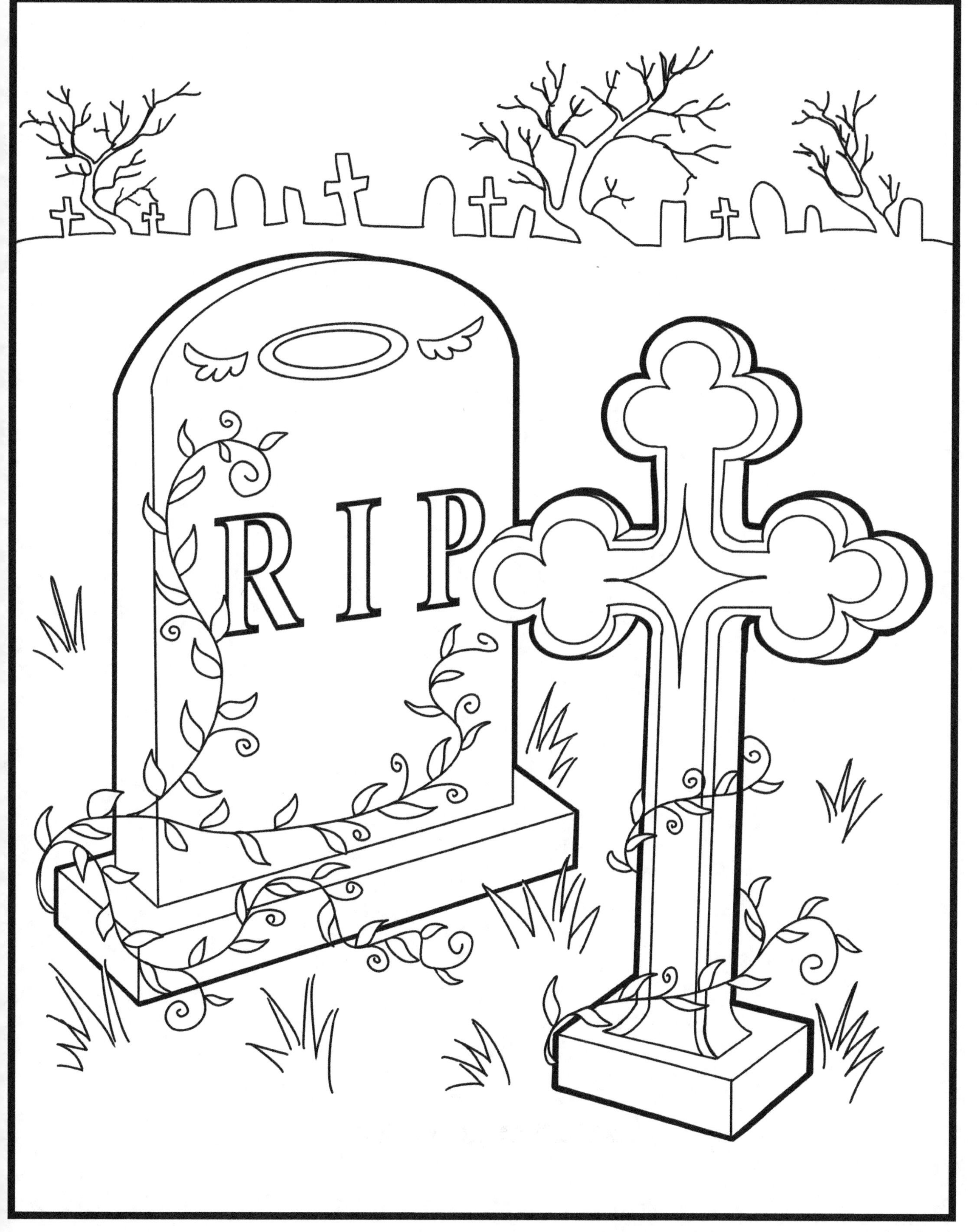

Grave Stones

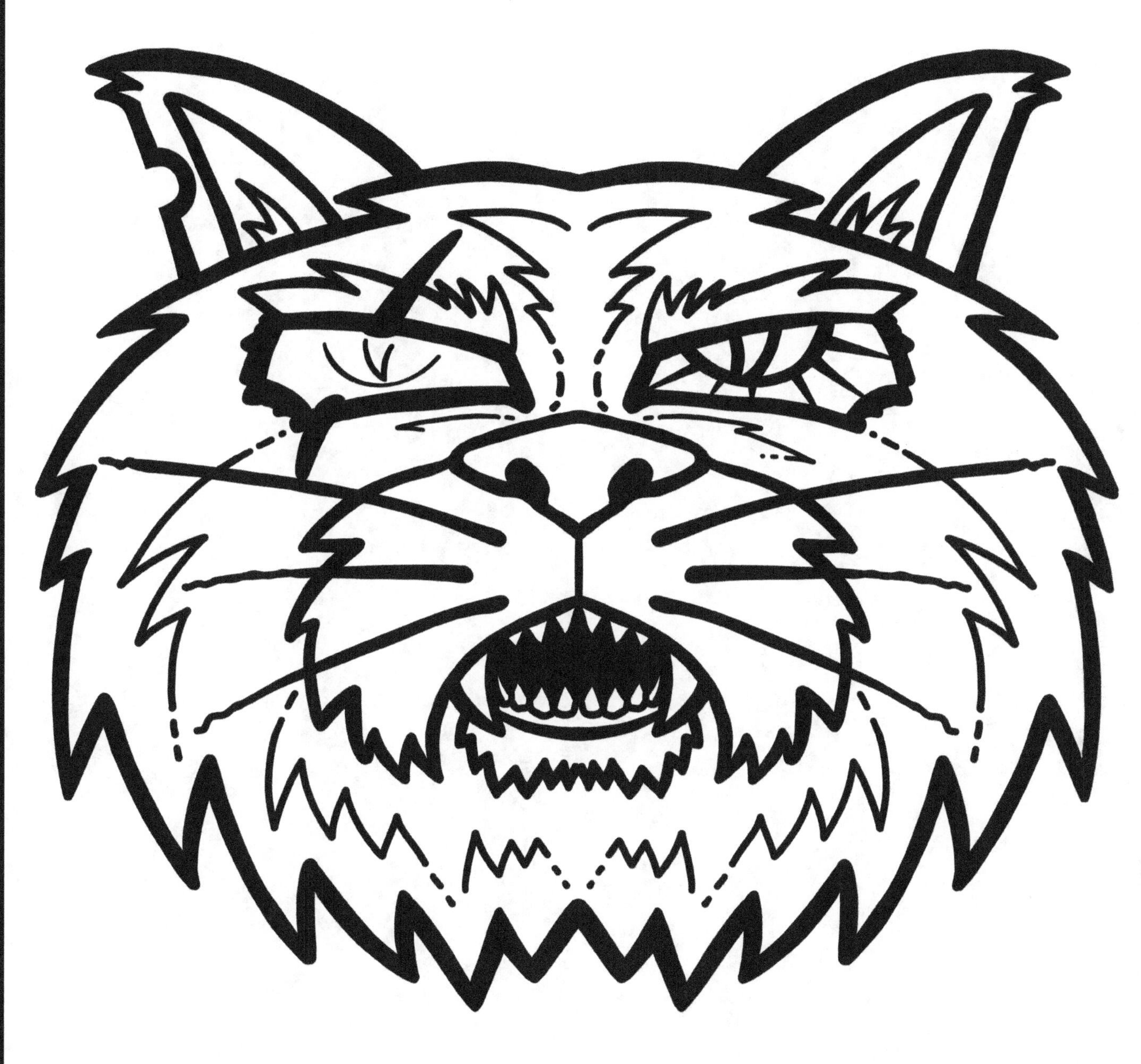

Killer Cat

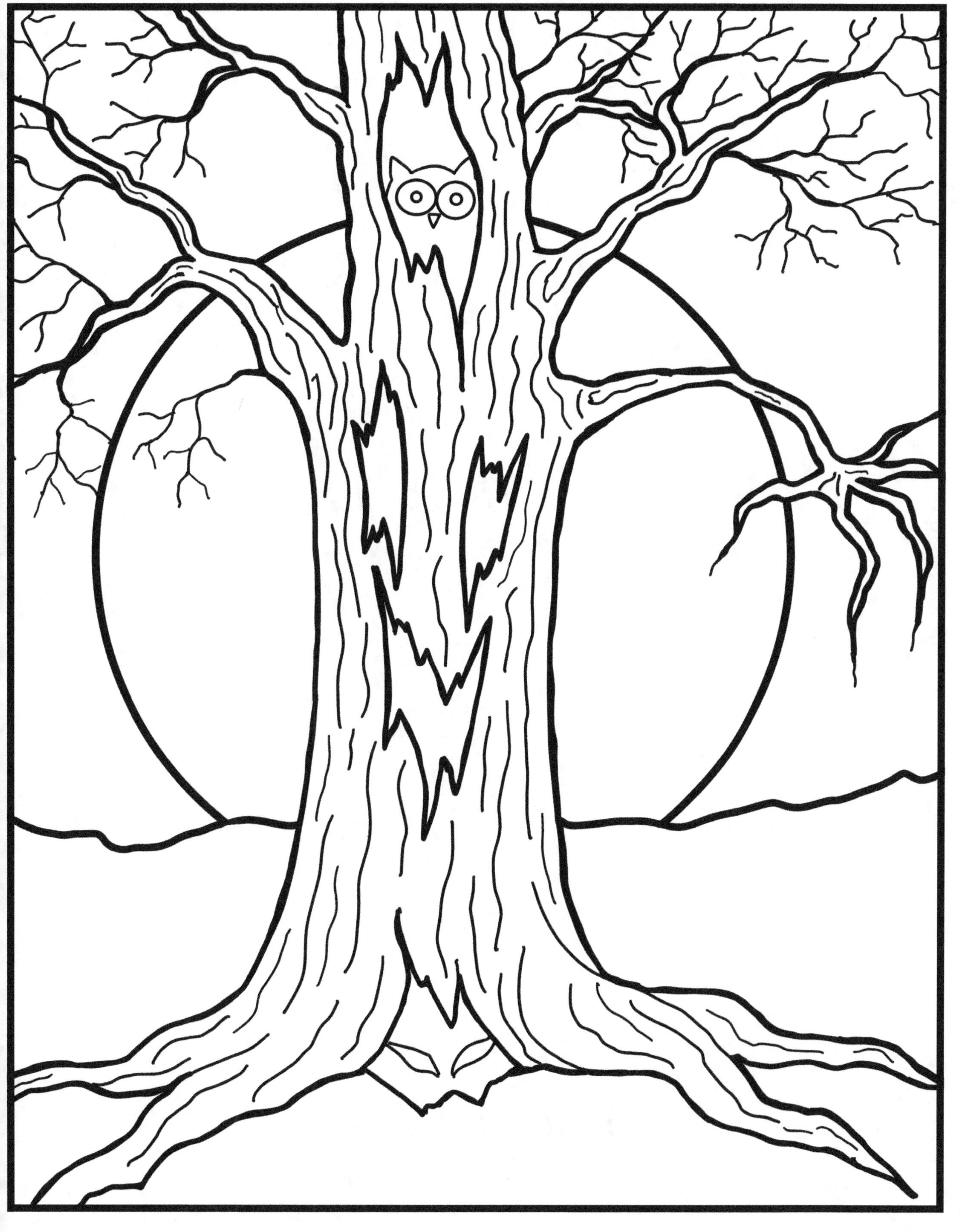

Haunted Tree

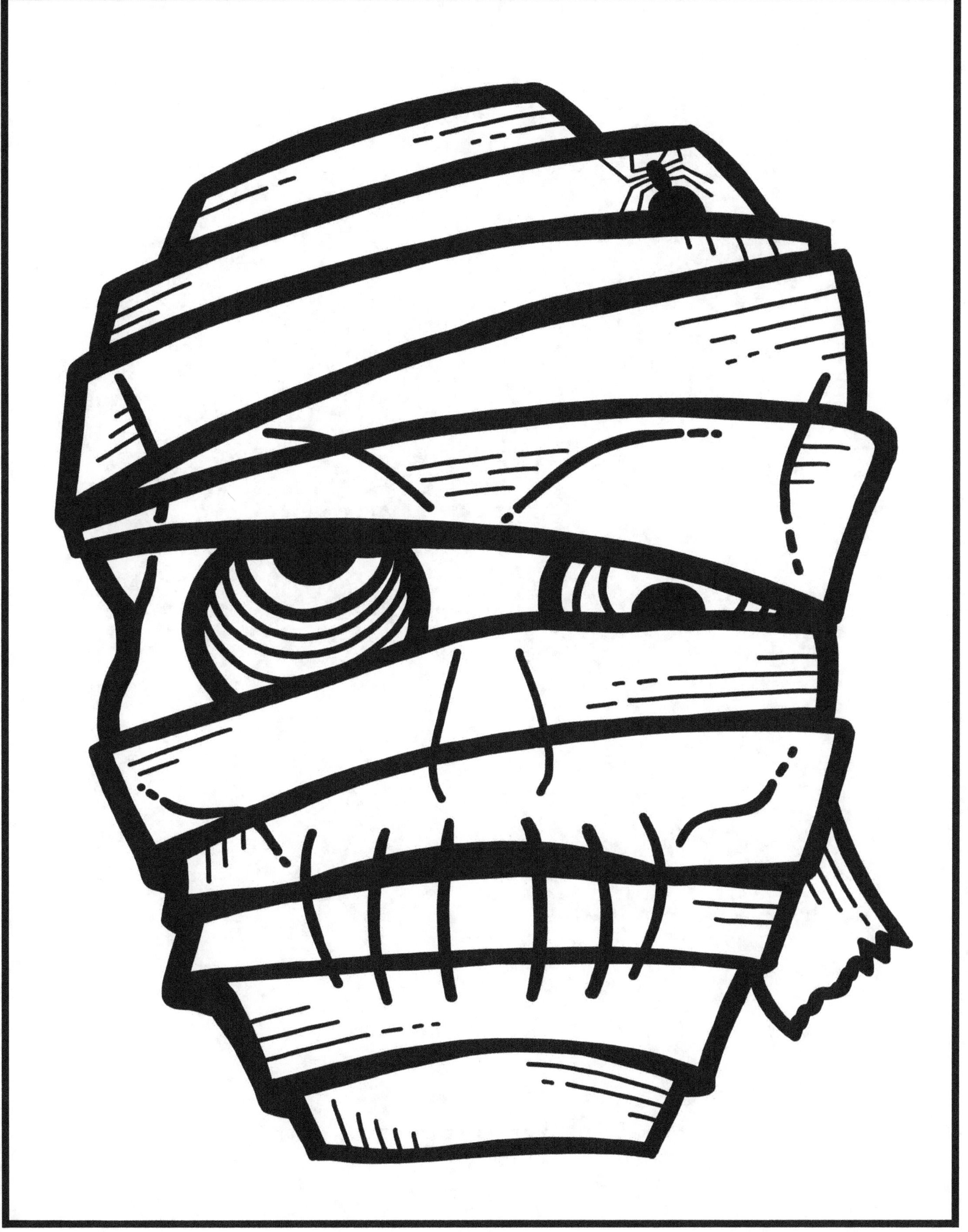

Mummy

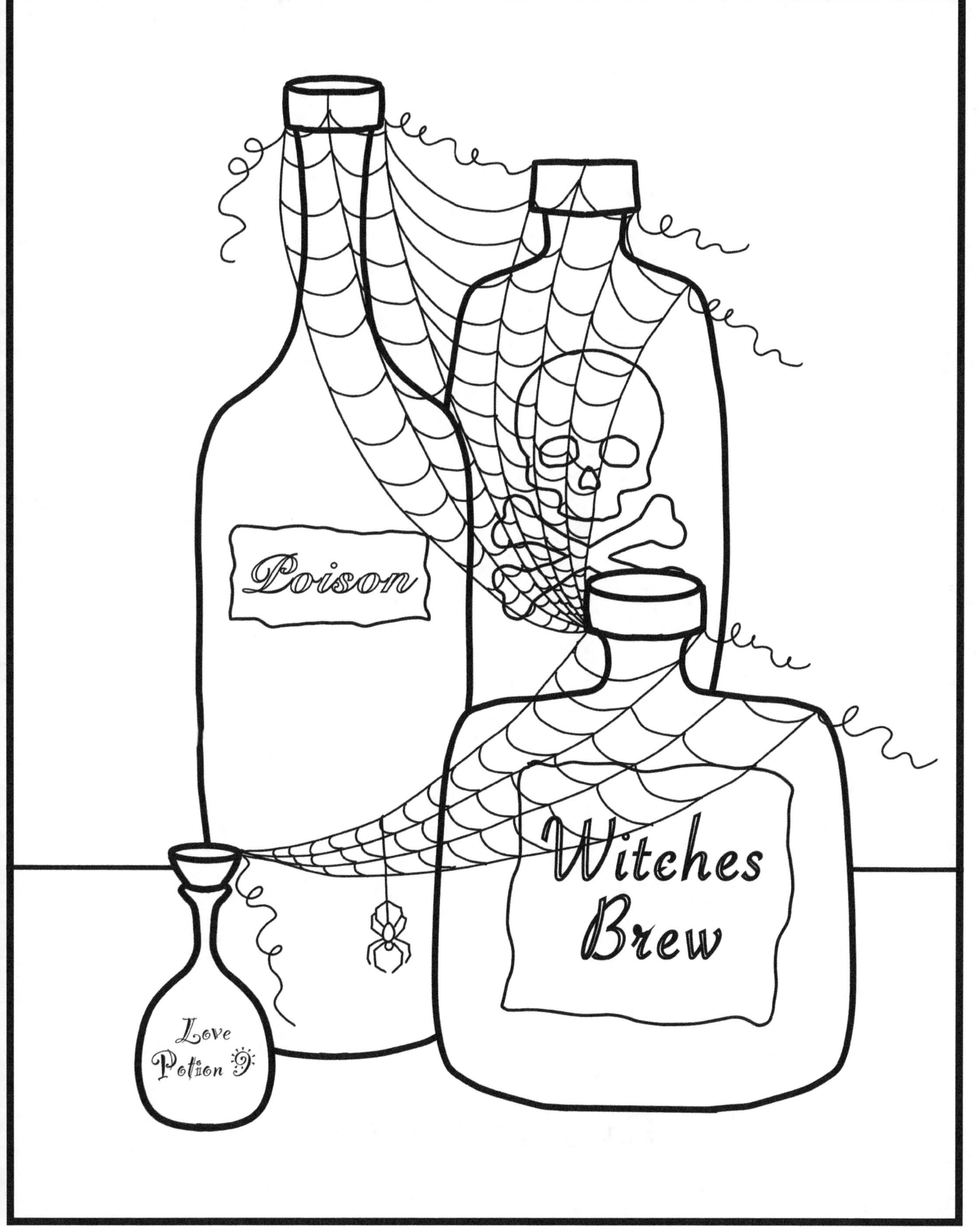

Poison
Witches
Brew
Love
Potion 9

Poison Bottles

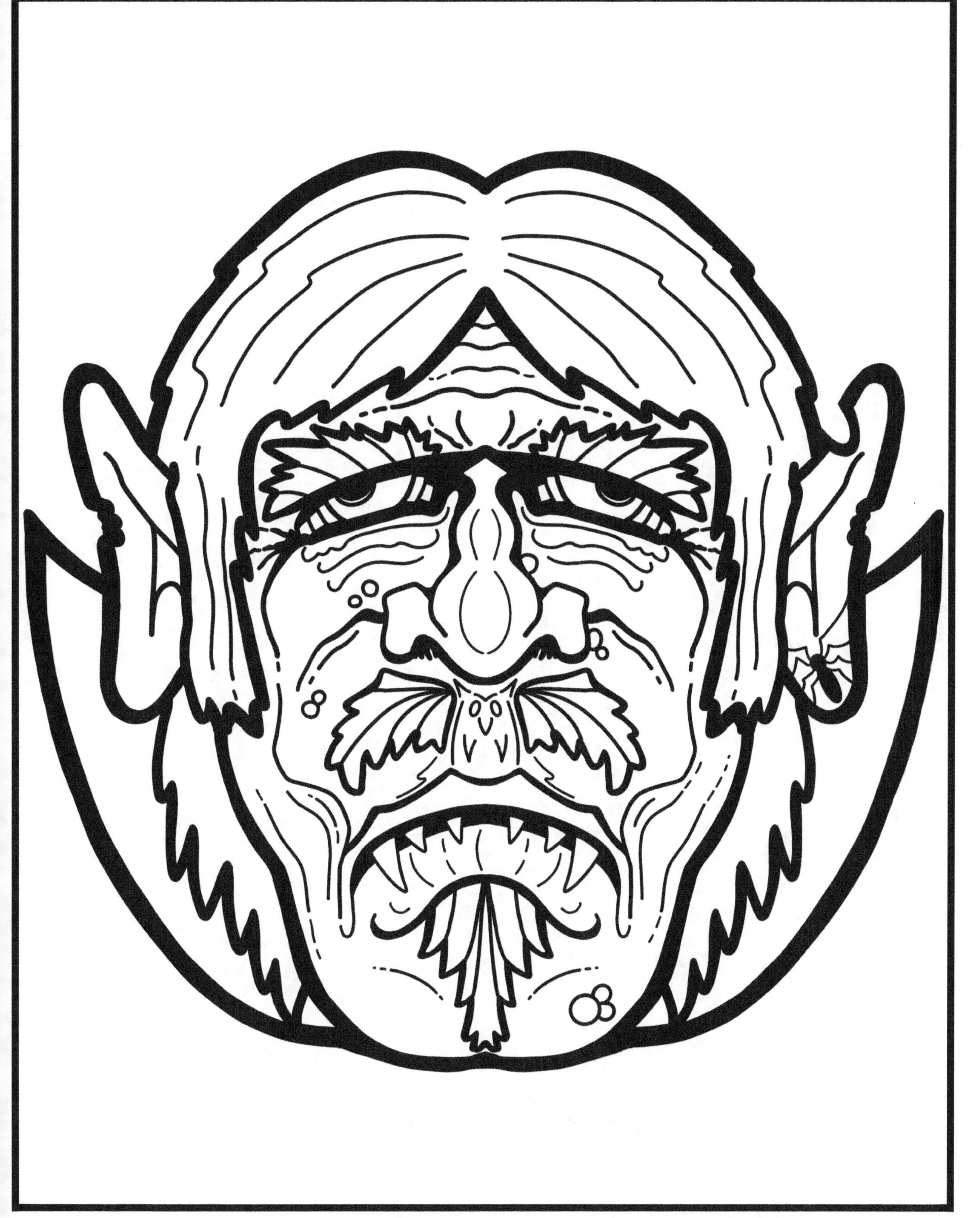

Very Old Vampire

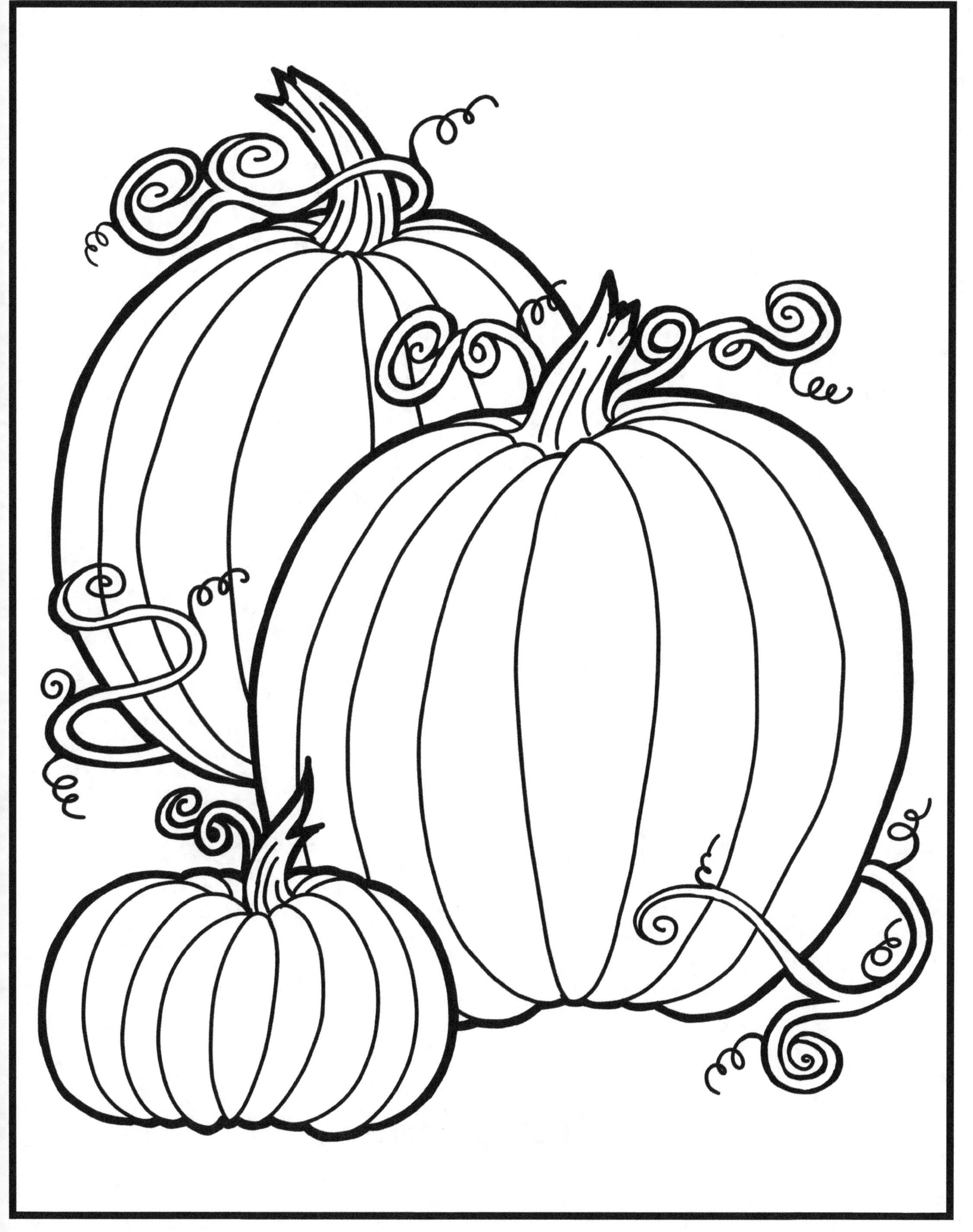

Pumpkins

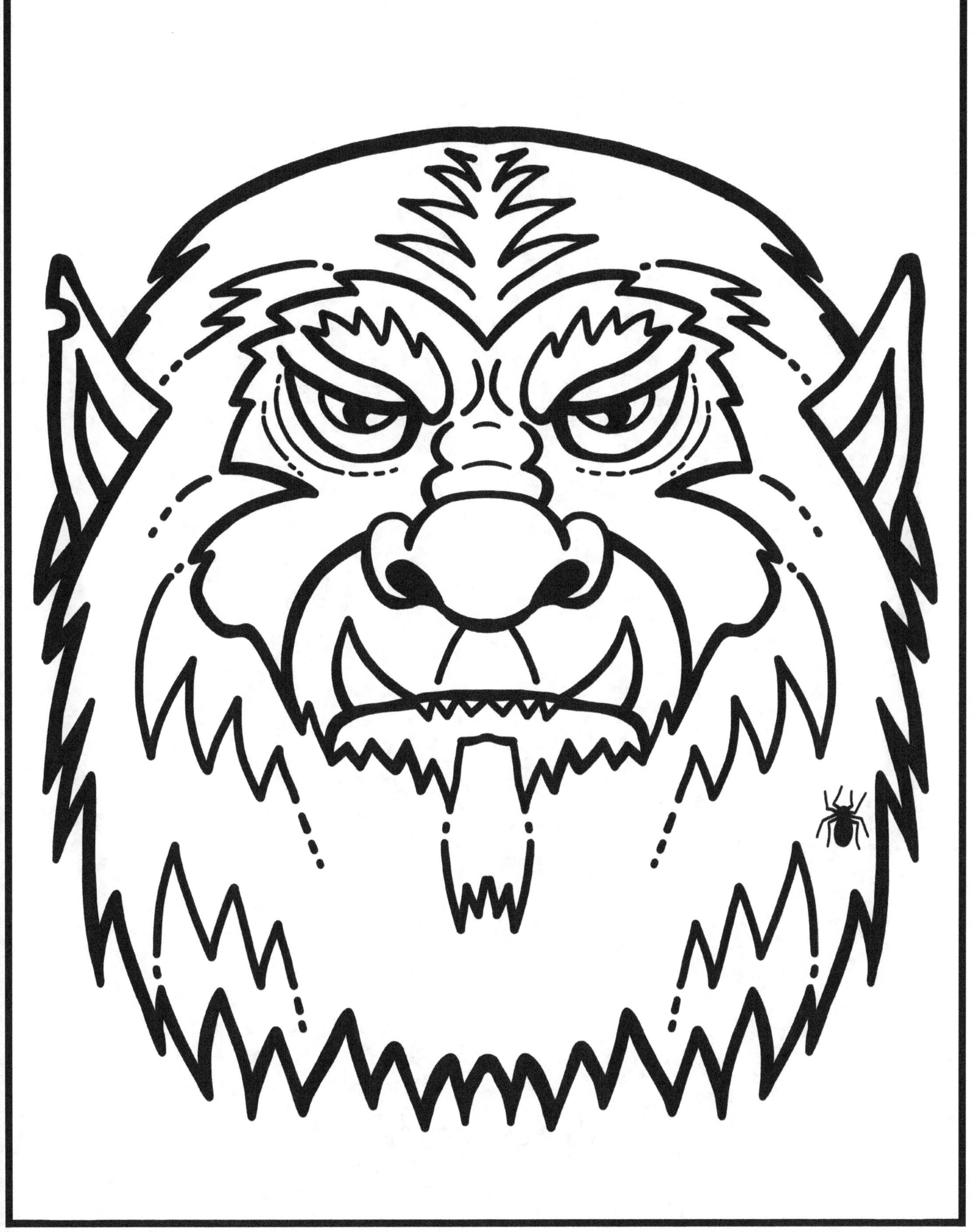

Werewolf

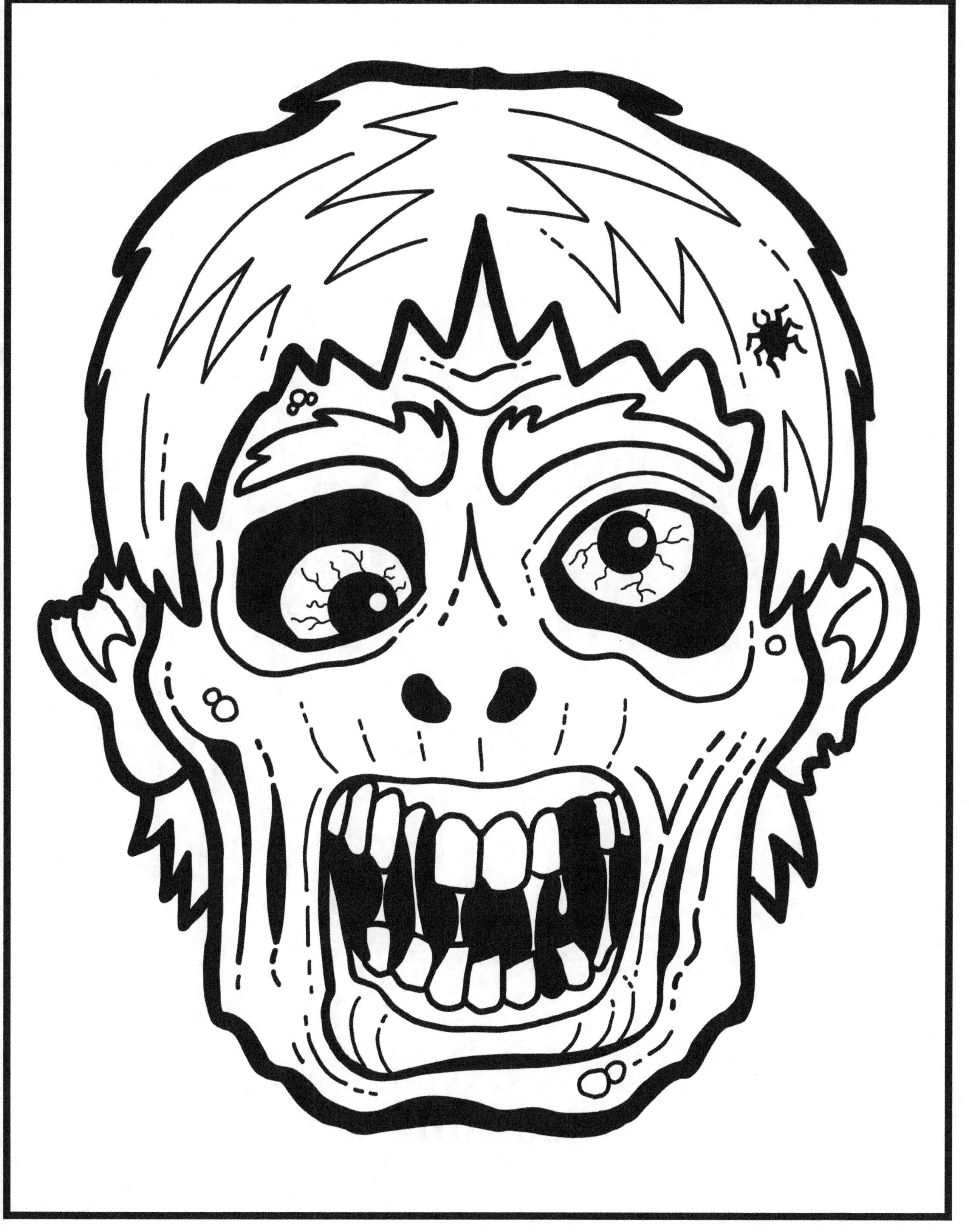

Zombie